The Really Easy Obo

Very first solos for oboe with piano accompaniment
Leichte Spielstücke für Oboe und Klavier
Tout premiers solos pour hautbois avec accompagnement pianistique

ROBERT HINCHLIFFE

© 1988 by Faber Music Ltd
First published in 1988 by Faber Music Ltd
Bloomsbury House 74–77 Great Russell Street London WC1B 3DA
Music engraved by Sambo Music Engraving Co
Cover illustration by John Levers
Printed in England by Caligraving Ltd
All rights reserved

ISBN10: 0-571-51033-7
EAN13: 978-0-571-51033-7

To buy Faber Music publications or to find out about the full range of titles available
please contact your local music retailer or Faber Music sales enquiries:

Faber Music Limited, Burnt Mill, Elizabeth Way, Harlow, CM20 2HX England
Tel: +44 (0)1279 82 89 82   Fax: +44 (0)1279 82 89 83
sales@fabermusic.com   fabermusic.com

Preface

You need only be able to play a few notes on the oboe to make music. The 20 little pieces in this book have been written with beginners in mind, but within the technical limitations this imposes there is plenty of scope for musical interest. The pieces are arranged progressively, so as well as musical satisfaction you can have the pleasure of hearing the step-by-step improvement in your playing. The piano accompaniments have been kept as simple as possible.

First Book of Oboe Solos and *Second Book of Oboe Solos* by Janet Craxton and Alan Richardson are also available.

Contents

1. March of the Ducks

© 1988 by Faber Music Ltd.

This music is copyright. Photocopying is illegal.

2. Daydreaming

Andante (♩ = 72)

3. Holiday Trot

Allegretto (♩ = 100)

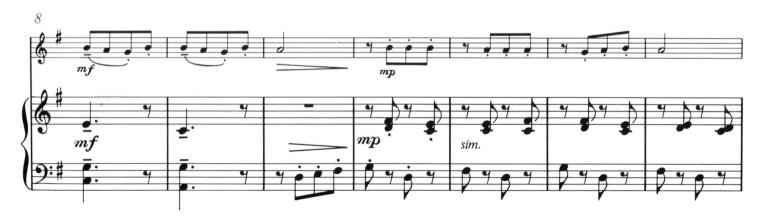

4. The Brook

4

5. Mellifluous Minuet

6. Nocturne

6

7. Spring Song

8. Elizabethan Lament

8

9. The Barrel Organ

Allegro giocoso (♪ = 138)

10. Siciliana

11.   Dance of the Scarecrows

12. Ballad

13.   Jovial Jig

14. Berceuse

15.   Children's March

Tempo giusto (♩ = 88)

16.   Wistful Waltz

17.   Christmas Song

18

18. Comedy

19. A Winter's Tale

20.   Country Dance

OBOE VOLUMES

from Faber Music

The *Really* Easy Oboe Book *Robert Hinchliffe*
ISBN 0-571-51033-7

Two by Two (oboe duets) *Robert Hinchliffe*
ISBN 0-571-51221-6

Oboe Carol Time *Robert Hinchliffe*
ISBN 0-571-51228-3

Improve your sight-reading! Grades 1–3 *Paul Harris*
ISBN 0-571-51633-5

Improve your sight-reading! Grades 4–5 *Paul Harris*
ISBN 0-571-51634-X

First Book of Oboe Solos *edited by Janet Craxton & Alan Richardson*
ISBN 0-571-50372-1

Second Book of Oboe Solos *edited by Janet Craxton & Alan Richardson*
ISBN 0-571-50328-4

Going Solo *edited by Sarah Francis & Robert Grant*
ISBN 0-571-51494-4

80 Graded Studies for Oboe. Book 1 *John Davies & Paul Harris*
ISBN 0-571-51175-9

80 Graded Studies for Oboe. Book 2 *John Davies & Paul Harris*
ISBN 0-571-51176-7

FABER *ff* MUSIC